The No Nonsense Guide to Recovery

BounceBack

FROM DEPRESSION

SHARON EDEN

RETHINK PRESS

First published in Great Britain 2015
by Rethink Press (www.rethinkpress.com)

Cover image © istockphoto.com/enviromantic

Praise for Bounce Back From Depression

'Congratulations! I found *Bounce Back from Depression* optimistic, down to earth, realistic and engaging. A book you can keep in your briefcase, or a handbag, and reference. I enjoyed your very readable style.'

Dorothy Dalton, CEO 3Plus International Ltd
Career & Leadership Coaching for High Potential Women
www.3plusinternational.com

'This book can help you see that you are more resilient and nearer Bounce Back than you think. It also courageously challenges the usual professional view of dealing with depression.'

Irene Brankin
Chartered Counselling Psychologist
Author of *The Visible Woman* and *I Don't Care!*
www.thevisiblewoman.com

'When you are depressed everything feels too difficult and too much effort. You feel as if nothing is going to help you out of the black cloud in which you exist. Sharon has put together an easy and practical guide you can dip intro that offers no nonsense, sensible advice: like a friend gently, yet firmly, saying, 'You can do this. I am right with you.' No frills, no fluff, just straight to the heart to get you back on track: to 'bounce back', I thoroughly recommend this book. Read it in bite sized chunks, return to it often and start to smile again.'

Dr Suzanne Henwood
mBIT Coach and Master Trainer
www.mBrainingf4Success.com

'Easy to read in an encouraging and friendly tone, Sharon normalises depression as part of life while tackling important issues like suicidal thoughts and medication. *Bounce Back From Depression* is a motivational and comprehensive recovery kit with useful links.'

Freda Child
Poet and artist

'Sharon's insightful approach to depression shatters myths, offers practical, no-nonsense approaches and comes from her own lived-it experience, both personally and as a Coach-Psychotherapist. Using some of Sharon's techniques to support a friend, I'm pleased to say they're working with, of course, my friend's commitment to get her life back. *Bounce Back* could work for you too.'

Phyllis Santamaria, PhD
Founder-Director of Learning Without Borders
www.learning-without-borders.com

'I am humbled by how very open and honest Sharon is about her personal experience of depression. She is clearly passionate about sharing her experience and learning with her audience and her clients so that they too can believe in their recovery from depression. The tips and techniques are easily accessible and extremely practical.'

Philomena Ovenden
Psychodynamic Counsellor, Psychotherapist,
Supervisor and EMDR Practitioner

'If it wasn't for depression, I wouldn't be who I am now. If it wasn't for depression, I wouldn't be working with what I am now. If it wasn't for depression, I wouldn't be living where I am now... and getting ready to move into my new home. It's the warmth and wisdom in Sharon's book that will grab you and stay with you as you find your way to bounce back from depression. Buy it. Read it. Treasure it.'

Lise Moen
Strategist and writer
www.lisemoen.com

'With exquisite clarity, this very important book rises from the wisdom and mystery born of authentic experience to disarm the complexities of depression. Sharon's great gift is a passionate and powerful guide which skilfully teaches us to see ourselves in new ways for empowerment, renewal and healing. Fabulous!'

Dr Jack King, CPL
Leadership Coach and Consultant, Public Servant
Author of *One with the People*
www.WalnutRidgeConsulting.com

For Alanna, Dayna, Naomi, Jaxon and Zachary

'Depression is withheld knowledge.'

John Layard

'In the midst of winter,
I found there was within me
an invincible summer.'

Albert Camus

CONTENTS

INTRODUCTION

My name is Sharon Eden and I'm a recovering depressive.

I was a depressed child, teenager and adult. Throw into the mix several dollops of trauma and suicidal episodes for good measure.

At best, the therapists I saw as an adult helped my depression lighten. At worst, their approach helped it to deepen. So, when I trained to become a psychotherapist in the early 1980s I was determined to research things which really would help me recover.

The good news is I found and invented lots of stuff which helped me and my clients recover, and continues to do so. A lot of that 'stuff' is here in this book.

It's a no nonsense, no punches pulled and basic recipe to help you recover from depression sooner rather than later. For, despite what you've been led to believe, you *can* bounce back from depression in weeks rather than months or years.

Loss of concentration and focus is usual when you're depressed. So this book is short, to the point and in easily digestible bits. In some sections, if you want to know more you can download extra information from my website.

Simple works so much better than complicated. Recovery from depression is simple if you co-operate with the way your body, feelings, mind and essential energy, your oomph, operate. Everything in this book is tailored to do just that.

Within these pages I challenge the established medical model of depression and how to treat it. As depression is now at epidemic levels and repeat prescriptions for antidepressants increasing year on year, clearly it's time for a new approach.

My approach is that depression is not an illness to be cured. It is part of the human condition to be embraced, leaned into and, in recovery, tapped for the personal growth which lies in its shadows.

This is your book. Feel free to turn down pages, write all over it and highlight whatever you want. If it ends up like a dish-cloth, so what? Squeeze every last drop of help from it in any way you can.

You *can* recover from depression... and much, much sooner than you think!

Sharon

1

DEPRESSION

1

1

DEPRESSION

A definition of depression

The *Oxford Dictionary* says depression is, 'A mental condition characterised by feelings of severe despondency and dejection, typically also with feelings of inadequacy and guilt, often accompanied by lack of energy and disturbance of appetite and sleep.'

You can experience ongoing, low-level depression, even from childhood, which becomes your 'normal' and lasts for ages, even lifetimes. You can experience depression on a scale of severity starting with 'moderate'. The most severe depression of all includes thoughts, feelings, urges and justifications about killing yourself. In extremis, you could commit suicide.

Causes of depression

Loss is a big cause of depression. For example, loss due to the break-up of a relationship, the death of a loved one, redundancy, retirement or the loss of your home.

There can also be a loss of your identity. The loss of who you thought you were through a particular role ending, like being a mother, husband, a 'good' person or a best friend. People who lose their job or retire can also become depressed through this kind of loss.

Those roles can be easily shattered. But dreams can also be broken and create a loss of something you wanted or expected but never had. For example, depression can be triggered by the ending of hopes and dreams like on-going romance, getting 'that' job, moving home or having a baby.

Life events and changes that might trigger depression include the menopause, financial difficulties, job problems, a medical diagnosis (e.g. cancer or HIV), bullying, natural disasters, social isolation, jealousy, separation, life-changing physical injuries or having a baby.

A client, diagnosed with Post Natal Depression, had thought with horror when she first held her baby, 'Life is never going to be the same again!' It's likely that those feelings of loss of freedom, and perhaps guilt about them, could have triggered her depression. For other women, childbirth can trigger emotional flashbacks from past traumas leading to depression.

Indeed, psychological issues like Post Traumatic Stress or Post Traumatic Stress Disorder and some personality disorders also involve depression.

It can also be a symptom of some medical conditions, or a side effect of some drugs or medical treatments. Some current ideas even suggest that some medical conditions like chronic fatigue syndrome might be depression expressed only through the body.

Some more definitions of depression

Here are some more ideas about what depression is. Tick the ones which feel right for you:

- A biochemical imbalance in the brain.

- Reactive depression is as a consequence of life events

- Endogenous depression is assumed to be something internal to the person

- A mood disorder

- Living dead

- Hell-on-two-wheels

- Part of the human condition

- A personal growth opportunity

- A dis-ease

- A crisis of meaning and purpose

- Facing up to the reality of your life

- 'The Dark Night of the soul' (poem by Saint John of the Cross)

- Your soul trying to get your attention

Some of the definitions might intuitively feel right for you even if you don't know why. For more information download '9 Alternative Definitions of Depression' from http://bouncebackuk.com/resources/

Symptoms of depression

Depression is a whole-person experience. That means you can have symptoms of it in your body, your feelings, your mind and your zest for life – your 'oomph' – whatever you believe your oomph to be.

Here are some symptoms. Tick the ones you're having now.

- Continuous low mood or sadness

- Feeling hopeless and helpless

- Feeling guilt and shame

- Feeling worthless

- Low self-esteem

- Tearfulness or all dried up

- Irritable

- Can't be bothered

- Unable to make decisions

- Anxious or worried

- Negative punishing thoughts

- Negative shaming thoughts

- 'It would be better not to wake up' thoughts

- Poor concentration and memory

- Eating more or less than normal

- Putting on or losing weight

- Digestive problems

- Lack of energy

- Lack of interest in sex

- Waking in the night

- Can't get to sleep

- Feeling exhausted when you wake up

- Withdrawing socially from friends and family

- Not doing well at work

- Having difficulties in your home and family life

- Nothing brings you enjoyment

- Everything's a catastrophe

- Self-harming

- Desire to kill yourself

- Working out how to kill yourself

- Feeling as if you are going mad

- Thinking you are mad

- The morning 'dreads'

- Sheer terror

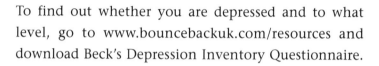

To find out whether you are depressed and to what level, go to www.bouncebackuk.com/resources and download Beck's Depression Inventory Questionnaire.

If you are suicidal, get medical care. Go to your GP, call your out of hours' service or go to A & E now. Samaritans can be a good support during this time. Go to www.samaritans.org.uk and find your nearest branch.

Wanting to kill yourself

When you're suicidal you need an emergency appointment. To get past the GP's gate keeper, otherwise known as 'the receptionist', say, 'My name is.......... I want to kill myself and need an urgent emergency appointment now please.'

I once wanted to kill myself and had worked out how to do it. At the very, very last moment, just as I was about to do it, I heard a deep yell of 'Nooooooo!' inside my head. Then, very briefly, I 'saw' a glimpse of a pop-band in my mind and heard a snatch of a song.

That sounds strange, doesn't it? But the experience stopped me in my tracks like I'd had a mega electrical shock. After a tortured night, I went straight to my GP early the next morning for emergency help.

Years later, I recognised that the band in my glimpse was The Communards. And the snatch of song?

'Don't leave me this way.
I can't survive, I can't stay alive,
Without your love.
... don't leave me this way.'

It goes beyond coincidence that I got this on the verge of killing myself. I believe it was an intervention from the spark of the divine within me, from my own Inner Wisdom.

I could have chosen not to listen. But I did, even though I didn't understand the images I got or what the snatch of song was about. How awesome that my inner voice stopped me. How awesome that I then took pro-life action rather than anti-life action, as I had intended.

For, if I'd chosen not to listen and killed myself, here's some of what I would have missed:

- My daughter's graduation from university

- My daughter's wedding

- Seeing Ben Haenow win *The X Factor* 2014

- My son's divorce and finding a loving partner

- My garden given feminine curves by my gardener

- The birth of my son's son and my daughter's daughter

- Exploring the Harry Potter studios with a great friend

- Watching some great rugby

- Being a student at The School for Wizards

- The joy of another grandchild born as I edited this book

- Meeting new friends whom I love

- Some tough times too, but also countless times of laughter, mischief and celebration, including those to come!

If you're intent on taking your life, there's no way I can stop you. But I know you will be dreadfully missed, even if you don't believe you will be as the anti-life gremlins in you suggest. Plus, you will miss so much from a future you'll never know.

Depression success stories

Here are some famous people who have experienced episodes of depression. Some of them still do.

Abraham Lincoln

Winston Churchill

Eleanor Roosevelt

Sigmund Freud

J K Rowling

Brook Shields

Charles Dickens

Joseph Conrad

Ernest Hemingway

Mark Twain

Stephen Fry

Angelina Jolie

Catherine Zeta Jones

Kylie Minogue

Sheryl Crow

Diana, Princess of Wales

Russell Brand

Tennessee Williams

Buzz Aldrin

Sir Isaac Newton

Dolly Parton

F. Scott Fitzgerald

Billy Joel

Harrison Ford

Brad Pitt

Oprah Winfrey

Research what they've done with their lives despite depression. Or, perhaps more correctly, because of it. Who knows?

Depression has certainly helped me become who I am today and led me to do the work I love. I wouldn't change that for the world.

Lean into your depression

Imagine you're snow-boarding on a mountain and you lose balance. The instinctive urge is to control the wobble; to fight to correct it. Yet that's the totally wrong thing to do.

The correct thing is to always focus on the mountain and when you wobble lean into it with your body. Self-correction then naturally happens.

It's the same with depression. Try to control or fight it and it only gets worse. So, lean into your depression as if it were that mountain. Embrace your depression.

Then, through your acceptance, depression softens. It still needs you to be active in your recovery and to explore the personal development lessons it can give you. But that's all part of the evolutionary journey depression offers you.

2

PASSION

2

PASSION

Why Passion?

It might feel strange to move straight from a chapter on depression to one on Passion. But that's because depression is the polar opposite of Passion. It's usually Passion-less. That's Passion-less for *anything* in your life, including you. So, here's a chance to see what you can reclaim as you recover from depression.

Definitions of Passion

Tick the answers which feel right for you. Passion is...

- Pro-life energy

- Enthusiasm pulsing through your veins

- Focused attention to get things done

- Loving what you're doing

- Getting lost in the flow of what you're doing.

- Deep love.

15

- Sexy (and not just in sex)

- Feeling at one with nature

- Bouncing out of bed on a good day

- Energy to carry on when the going is tough

- Energy to enjoy

- A creativity flow

- Add some definitions of your own here...

-

-

-

-

-

What is Passion?

Passion with a capital P is your essential pro-life energy and your absolute birthright and heritage.

It's the parent of your enthusiasm, vitality and up-for-it-ness. It brings a feeling of wellbeing which, in the extreme, feels like every cell in your body is tingling.

Your passions with a small 'p' are the things you love to do and will spend time, energy, effort and even money on. Your passions can include your work, hobbies, going to the theatre, watching football, dancing, skateboarding or whatever. What are your passions when you're feeling full of ooomph?

Passion with a capital P is your 1000% atom-splitting life energy. Remember a time when you were full of Passion. In your memory, feel your Passion again, if only for a nano-second. It's still within and waiting for you.

Passion has a direct line to your spirituality and your Soul. It harnesses the power of your Inner Wisdom and, at the same time, that of the Universe.

If you believe you are just a body, feelings and mind, please stretch your imagination because I am sure there have been times in your life when you felt something else beyond. Perhaps that was a time when you were filled with overwhelming joy in nature, or holding a newborn baby, or the magnificence of a sunrise or sunset.

At such times, I believe you connect with the divine both within and outside of yourself. I also believe that Passion has a direct line to the divine, harnessing the power of your Inner Wisdom and, at the same time, that of the Universe.

If you've ticked some of the answers that describe what Passion is, you'll have a 'knowing' that your Passion is indeed way more than any-old-every-day energy.

The Pro-life Power of Passion

You can use the pro-life power of your Passion through action.

You know when you wake up with 'the dreads' and just don't want to face the world? Use your Passion, however weak or non-existent you think it is, to make an act of willpower.

Get up and brush those teeth. Then wash your face. Then brush your hair. Each small act of willpower to create an action is a step toward coming 'alive' *and* your bounce back from depression.

I once worked with a schoolteacher who was very depressed and anxious. He didn't enjoy teaching. What he loved (his passion with a small p) was working with his hands. He loved building, decorating and all things electrical and plumbing.

He bought a very cheap, rundown and small property and made many acts of willpower to renovate it in his spare time. Guess what? By taking action through his passion of working with his hands, even when he didn't feel like it, he connected more and more with his capital P Passion.

As he connected more with the pro-life energy of his Passion, he began to bounce back. In a very short space of time his depression and anxiety subsided.

We'll return to Passion in action later. However, you don't have to buy a house to renovate. Your everyday small acts of willpower, like washing up your mug or toasting some bread, will help re-connect, over time, with your Passion; your own essential pro-life energy.

Even making the bed when you really-really-really don't want to!

More on the relationship between depression and Passion

Depression feels like Elvis has just left the building. There's no buzz or interest or va va va voom.

Your anti-life depression gremlins can make things life-less. Everything can feel insurmountable: a mountain to climb. If only you could find the first foothold.

Well, while there's life there's most definitely hope. And, as Passion is the spring from which both life and hope flow, even if you're not feeling alive and hopeful right now, Passion can help you climb that mountain.

How to re-connect with your Passion

You might feel you've totally lost your Passion; your pro-life positive energy. But you haven't. It's always, but always, just a hair's breadth away. How do I know? Find out, by making at least one of the following acts of willpower.

19

- Quickly jump up and down on the spot 10 times.

- Be on the lookout for moments, even nano-seconds, of connection with your Passion. A glint of sun on the road, the sweet smell of a flower, the touch of a child or loved one, the sudden smell of home cooking, or whatever.

- Let yourself sob. There's pro-life energy in sobbing noises and tears. At the very least, crying releases stress hormones through your tears.

- Explore with your eyes a painting, photograph or picture which has had deep meaning for you.

- Imagine being in a beautiful, safe place in nature and explore it with all your senses. Go to www.bouncebackuk.com/resources and download the 'You Were Meant to Hang Loose' pdf.

How to connect with your pro-life Passion can be a very personal thing. One way which works for me is through playing upbeat pop music. No sad lyrics, please. For others, classical overtures with positive sentiments might be just the thing.

Here's another way to reconnect with your Passion:

Remember a time when you were on top of the world and feeling full of life. When was that? Where were you? What were you doing? Who were you with, if anyone?

Create a mental snapshot of this time. Imagine physically clicking a camera's button to capture this time. You too can be a David Bailey in your imagination.

Repeat this process twice more with different memories. Then create a mental memory snapshot sequence as if you had a little album of these feeling-full-of-life times.

As the images in your mind evoke feelings, use your 'album' to reconnect with your Passion again and again. That might happen immediately or bit by bit as you repeatedly run your good time snapshot sequence.

Which activity on these pages best helped you to reconnect you with your Passion, even for a moment? And why not create some of your own? Kicking a ball round the garden, planning something you'd normally love doing or singing vigorously and loudly.

Connecting with your Passion, however slowly, will help you bounce back from depression sooner rather than later. I promise!

3

MEDICATION

3

MEDICATION

Caution

If you are already taking anti-depressants and/or medication for manic depression, bi-polar personality disorder or a psychotic condition...

KEEP TAKING THE MEDICATION

Any change needs discussion with and monitoring by your GP or psychiatrist. If you stop taking your medication suddenly you could induce a kick-back depression... or worse.

Medication is not for messing with, particularly if you're taking it for one of the above conditions. Withdrawal will end up with you out of control. Not a great place to be.

Antidepressants

It's always your choice whether you take antidepressants or not. However, if you're feeling suicidal your GP might recommend medication. Apart from the risk to your life, feeling suicidal is like being in the worst kind of hell you can imagine. And there's no way you can tap into the lessons depression can give you when you're being torn limb from limb by suicidal anti-life energy.

Increasingly, research evidence is showing that modern antidepressants (SSRIs) work only slightly better than a sugar pill. The difference is so small scientifically that it suggests these medications don't work. Even other medications, meant for other medical conditions and not depression, show the same kind of effectiveness as antidepressants.

This all sounds a bit barmy but what might be causing approximately 27% of people on antidepressants to recover could be:

- You're told it will help you recover and believing what you're told makes it so.

- By taking the antidepressant you feel you're taking control and helping yourself.

The holistic approach

Taking control and helping yourself is an excellent way to encourage recovery. Indeed, the whole purpose of this book is to get you active in your own bounce back, and taking charge recharges your pro-life battery bit by bit.

The most effective way of recovering from depression, and learning about the goodies it has to offer you, is through a holistic approach. This means you consciously do things not just to help your mental state (mind) but the whole of you.

And the whole of you includes your feelings, mind, your physicality (body), oomph, spirit, Soul and anything else you recognise as a part of you. It just makes sense that the more of you you work with for recovery, the more powerful the effect.

Here are some ideas that you could use:

- You breathe shallowly when stressed or depressed which starves your body and brain of oxygen. So, take at least two brisk, swinging arm walks of at least 15 minutes every day to make sure you get enough. (Body)

- Pretend to be a scientist. Spend time every day closely observing an object at different angles, counting any regular patterns (like shoelace holes in your trainers), and describing the object (like how big/small, its colours and features). This helps to start engaging your concentration and focus again. (Mind)

- Do something which would normally be pleasing for you, like buying fresh flowers for yourself, or a particular magazine, or a treat, or doing a small thing associated with your hobbies, if you have any. (Feelings)

- Do something spiritually uplifting like reading inspiring quotations, spending time quietly in nature, visiting art galleries or going to a concert. (Ooomph, spirit, Soul or whatever you call it)

Keep taking the medication

All of that doesn't mean you should *not* take prescribed antidepressants. If you feel they're working for you, keep taking them. Plus, it can be dangerous to stop taking them abruptly, as I mentioned before.

Sudden removal of the chemicals in your body might create a 'kick back' depression with the chance that your mood could alter and even produce aggressive effects. Your GP can advise you on how to wean yourself off antidepressants, slowly and safely.

Side effects

If you're taking antidepressants, beware of side effects. Read the leaflet in the packet in which they came. The leaflet has to include even the very rare side-effects. So, don't get paranoid. The rare side-effect won't necessarily happen to you but it's important to be aware that it could.

Some side-effects of some anti-depressants actually mimic symptoms of depression. Why would anyone create a medication to help you recover from depression which mimics depression? It's beyond me.

So, if you are getting, or have noticed any of the following symptoms getting worse, that might be due to your anti-depressant rather than your condition:

- the shakes

- anxiety

- weight changes

- aggression

- constipation

- insomnia

- palpitations

- confusion unsteadiness on your feet

- suicidal thoughts

- paranoia

If so, go back to your GP and ask for a change in medication.

If you feel suicidal when taking your medication, and you weren't before, that could also be a side-effect of the anti-depressant you are taking.

DO NOT WAIT. GET BACK TO YOUR GP OR PSYCHIATRIST NOW. TELL THEM WHAT'S HAPPENING AND DON'T BE FOBBED OFF. IF NEEDED, TAKE SOMEONE WITH YOU WHO CAN DO THE TALKING FOR YOU.

If you don't understand their answers, ask them to explain more clearly. Don't just accept that it might be your depression rather than the medication.

It could be, but who the hell wants to take a chance on it? Demand that they change your medication to one that doesn't have suicidal thoughts as a possible side effect.

If you need support, show your GP or psychiatrist these pages.

Beware of addiction

While it is claimed that modern antidepressants are not addictive, the fact is they are psychologically, even if not chemically. They can link into magical thinking like, 'Without them I'll go down the plug hole again.'

Sleeping pills

AVOID 'SLEEPING PILLS' LIKE THE PLAGUE

I haven't yet had a client for whom sleeping pills worked. Even if they do, they can make you feel like crap. They are also highly addictive. You don't need that on top of every-thing else. I'll be telling you later about some alternative and natural remedies to help get good quality sleep.

If you need support about sleeping pills, show your GP or psychiatrist the above.

Your part in things

Too often I work with someone who has been taking anti-depressants for years, with little improvement. Sometimes I work with people who have tried several anti-depressants over time, with little improvement.

We now know from the research that they don't cure depression. The secret is:

Medication on its own won't do it!

The only way to recover and bounce back is through being active in your own recovery. It needs butt-into-gear stuff from you. Even a tiny baby-step forward is a great start.

If you haven't started yet, you can always start now

And now and now and now... and *now*. Create a forward-moving force: a momentum which helps your recovery and bounce back.

If you blip, forget or can't be bothered some days, be gentle with yourself. And what do you do then? Just carry on moving forward moment by moment, action by action.

4

ALTERNATIVE AND NATURAL REMEDIES

4

ALTERNATIVE AND NATURAL REMEDIES

Caution

When you explore alternative and natural remedies, visit a well-established health food shop with well trained staff. Tell them your symptom/s and ask what products they and other customers think work the best for those symptoms.

It's always good to run what you intend to take past your GP. Be aware that some GPs have no knowledge of alternative remedies and may pooh-pooh the whole idea.

Don't be put off. Unless there's evidence what you intend to take is harmful, it's your choice about what you put or don't put into your body.

Pick-me-ups

You might like to take an old fashioned herbal and vitamin pick-me-up such as Floradix or Metatone, which can help as part of your bounce back. They're available in large supermarkets, many chemists and health food shops.

Herbal tablets

As a recovering depressive, I've found herbal tablets that relieve stress helpful. My favourite is Quiet Life. They're available in any large pharmacy, including in supermarkets, or online. They helped me manage anxiety and agitation when I gave up smoking decades ago, and generally help when my sleep is disrupted.

Valerian is a herb widely associated with improving sleep. As its tea tastes like what I imagine cat's pee would taste like, I highly recommend you buy Valerian in capsule or pill form.

You might need to experiment to find the brand of herbal tablet that works for you. However, they're all non-addictive. As you recover, you automatically stop using them. That's also true of the suggested remedies which follow.

For some people, herbal tablets work straight away. Other people, like me, require several doses before things start to improve.

DO NOT TAKE ST JOHN'S WORT IF YOU'RE TAKING PRESCRIBED MEDICATION OF ANY SORT.

St John's Wort can stop your medication working and cause harm. Research has shown it has no effect on established depression. So you might consider taking one of the following remedies instead.

Remedies

Some people, me included, find Dr Bach's Remedies help them bounce back from depression. My favourite is Star of Bethlehem, a remedy for shock, historic or current trauma. However, clients who remember no trauma in their lives seem also to benefit from the remedy.

The bottle says to dilute the remedy in water. Mainlining works better for me – at least four drops under the tongue at least four times a day to be effective! Use it as many times a day as you want. It's not addictive. And you will automatically use the remedy less and less as you recover, until not at all.

Similarly, Sweet Chestnut helps many people. It's a remedy for feeling at the end of the line and full of despair.

You can find out more about Dr Bach's remedies by going to www.bachcentre.com

Lastly, you might like to experiment with jasmine essential oil. It's a remedy for depression and for sleep disturbances among many other things.

Frankincense essential oil promotes deep breathing and relaxation. It can open your breathing passages and reduce blood pressure, moving your mental state back to calmness. I use it when sleep eludes me due to a busy mind.

ESSENTIAL OILS MUST NOT TO BE TAKEN ORALLY. THEY CAN CREATE HARM TAKEN THIS WAY.

Instead, put a very small dab on each side of your pillow and one on your duvet at night. You could also dab it onto a handkerchief to smell during the day or burn it in an essential oil burner.

Pregnant women should avoid using jasmine oil since it's a herb which stimulates blood flow in the pelvic area and uterus and can initiate menstruation.

Also, it's highly relaxing and sedating, so just a very small amount will work, rather than a lot which could knock you out.

Another oil which can help sleep disturbance is lavender (used as above). Its calming effect on the nervous system makes it useful to help with depression and anxiety too.

Pregnant and breastfeeding women should avoid using lavender essential oil. It's also recommended that diabetics stay away from lavender oil. And, like jasmine, only use a very small amount.

All of these remedies are available in health food shops and online. For more information, go to www.organic-facts.net

Vitamins and supplements

Consider taking multi-vitamins and minerals if you haven't been eating healthily for some time. Check that the supplement you choose contains the full range of the Vitamin B Complex, which helps certain brain functions work smoothly.

If you don't need a multi-vitamin and minerals tablet, get yourself B Complex which helps regulate mood and supports cognition. Foods which contain B Complex include:

- Poultry

- Eggs

- Yoghurt

- Leafy greens

Omega 3 can help lessen depression through reducing certain kinds of inflammation. It also helps lower the risk of heart problems – so it's a winner one way or another. It is found naturally in foods such as:

- oily fish, such as salmon, sardines and mackerel

- eggs

- shellfish

- pumpkin

- sunflower seeds

While there's no scientific evidence, it's thought that the inclusion of Vitamin D3 in your diet can help with depression. The most obvious source is sunlight. However, apart from tablets you can also get Vitamin D3 through eating the following foods:

- oily fish such as salmon, sardines and mackerel

- eggs

- fortified fat spreads

- fortified breakfast cereals

- powdered milk

Natural mood boosters

Vigorous physical exercise creates the release of feel-good chemicals in your body and alleviates stress. This boosts your mood naturally.

I know some mornings it's as much as you can do to get out of bed, let alone go for a walk. Yet inactivity is part of and sustains your depression. So get your butt into gear as part of your recovery bounce back routine.

Sometimes this demands an act of willpower where you have to make yourself do something physical when you really don't want to. Recap on how to do this by re-reading the 'pro-life power of Passion' section in Chapter 2.

Also, recognise that the part of you saying 'I can't be bothered' is an anti-life energy gremlin. While the part of you urging you to move your body is your Passion: delicious pro-life energy supporting your bounce back.

Schedule in two 15-minute brisk, arm-swinging walks a day. You'll raise those feel-good chemicals, get some oxygen into your bloodstream and create some physical tiredness to help sleep happen. Focusing on exercise can also distract you from negative thoughts and feelings.

Finally...

Research shows dancing is the fastest way to boost your mood

During my last bout of depression I played Kelly Clarkson or Meatloaf very loudly in my kitchen. Then I danced and wiggled and whooped until I was breathless. Sheer magic.

Remember, inactivity is part of your depression and sustains it. So, do get your butt moving for both the short and long-term benefits which help your recovery.

5

ADDICTIONS AND LEARNED BEHAVIOUR

5

ADDICTIONS AND LEARNED BEHAVIOUR

Alcohol

AVOID ALCOHOL LIKE THE PLAGUE!

Alcohol is itself a depressant. It only makes your depression worse.

I know it blurs the edges of your depression. But the price you pay is potentially making your depression even deeper and darker, and delaying your recovery.

Is prolonging your depression worth a very, very brief numbing from it?

STOP IT NOW!

If you're used to drinking alcohol, start keeping non-alcoholic drinks in your fridge and in your drinks cupboard. When you get the urge, drink one of those.

If you feel unable to stop drinking alcohol right now, start watering it down by 25%, then 50%, then 75%, then 100%.

If you feel unable to even do that, seek help. You might have become alcohol-dependent. Contact Alcoholics Anonymous (AA) www.alcoholics-anonymous.org.uk for support groups in your area, or other areas if you prefer. Find out from your GP about other local organisations that could also help.

Caffeine withdrawal symptoms

AVOID CAFFEINE LIKE THE PLAGUE!

Caffeine is a stimulant which makes your anxiety and agitation worse.

I know it gives you a boost. The price you pay is not just to boost your anxiety and agitation but to make them even worse. Recovery and your bounce back are delayed.

Is making your agitation and anxiety worse worth a momentary chemical high?

STOP IT NOW!

I've lost count of how many of my clients felt so much better just through taking caffeine out of their diet.

Go straight to decaf coffee and tea or teabags. Cut out

fizzy drinks with caffeine in them, too. Check all drinks and food labels to make sure they're caffeine-free.

If you feel unable to stop right now, use half a teaspoon of caffeinated and half a teaspoon of decaffeinated coffee per cup. Gradually decrease the caffeinated and increase the decaf until you're 100%. Half-and-half tea is one bag of each in a 2-cup teapot. I'm afraid it's cold turkey after that.

Chocolate

AVOID CHOCOLATE LIKE THE... OH DEAR!

If you love chocolate as I do, I'm sorry to tell you it contains a chemical almost identical to caffeine. It also contains a substance that creates a hit on the pleasure centre of your brain and an oh-this-is-so-delicious enjoyment spike.

However, your 'Mmmm' is very short-lived. As soon as the hit wears off, you crash again. Your desire for chocolate returns almost immediately. All of this creates an up-and-down agitation experience on top of being depressed.

Indeed, caffeine and its close relations can cause or contribute to imperfect balance, racing heart, insomnia and sleep disturbances, bed-wetting, fatigue, obesity, dizziness, irritability, agitation and anxiety, for example. Some diseases and health problems, including heart disease, allergies, diabetes, stomach disturbances, and depression can be made worse by these substances as well.

STOP IT NOW!

If you feel unable to stop chocolate straight away, wean yourself off. Buy organic and the darkest chocolate you can. At least they're better for you than brands with loads of chemicals in them.

Break the chocolate into small pieces and put them in the freezer in a plastic bag or box. Take out one frozen piece when necessary. It will take longer to melt in your mouth and you'll feel satisfied for longer.

Smoking nicotine

SMOKING NICOTINE IS ANOTHER NO-NO!

I know you think it relaxes you. In fact, that's because you suck in oxygen when you take your first drag. But nicotine is itself a stimulant. It only makes your anxiety and agitation worse, interferes with sleep and increases your stress hormones.

STOP IT NOW!

Nicotine and the chemicals in cigarettes rob your body of oxygen, which is essential to healing. You need every bit of oxygen you can get to help yourself bounce back.

As an ex-smoker, I know how hard it is to stop when you're *not* feeling depressed let alone when you are. Although you might be different from me.

I once knew a woman who successfully lost weight and gave up smoking at the same time even though she was experiencing depression. She reckoned if she did it all in one go the worst would be over soon. She had more whatever-it-takes-to-stop-smoking than me, for sure. If you can stop now, good for you.

For help, visit your GP and/or join the NHS quit smoking campaign http://www.nhs.uk/smokefree If appropriate, your GP might prescribe some medication to help.

Any other stuff

IF YOU ARE SMOKING, SNIFFING, SNORTING OR INJECTING ANY OTHER STUFF... STOP IT NOW!

Mood-altering drugs are dangerous, and even more so when you're depressed. Through using them you could be the one who develops a drug-induced psychosis like paranoia or a psychological disorder like schizophrenia.

I know it feels absolutely and horrendously impossible to stop if you're an addict. But if Russell Brand could come off and stay off that junk one day at a time, with support, so can you.

Get help!

First port of call is your GP, who will have information about services you can use to support you in coming off the stuff.

Part of coming clean is hanging around with people who are not using stuff and those committed to getting clean. Go to http://ukna.org/ for Narcotics Anonymous groups in your area, or, if you prefer, in other areas too.

Avoid foods like sugar

AVOID FOODS YOUR BODY ABSORBS QUICKLY LIKE THE PLAGUE!

These include foods such as sugar (more addictive than heroin), white bread (sugar in that too) or anything refined. That includes junk food.

I know it seems like they have a feel-good factor. That's because they give you a sugar high, but your blood sugars crash soon after you've eaten them. This makes you feel even more tired, lethargic and low than you were already.

STOP IT NOW!

To keep your blood sugars steady and avoid mood swings, eat foods which the body absorbs slowly. So, eat more wholegrain cereals and bread, pulses, fruit and vegetables. They're also filling and boost your energy levels.

Choose high fibre and low sugar wholegrain cereals. Have brown rice or yams instead of white rice and potatoes.

There's more information about food that helps you bounce back from depression in the next chapter on diet.

Learned behaviours

You're not weak if you find stopping alcohol, caffeine, nicotine or other stuff difficult. They're learned behaviours, ones which became habits and then addictions. Learning new behaviours to put in their place can help.

If part of you says, 'I can't stop ever', or 'Sure I can stop, but I don't want to', your habit has turned into an addiction. You feel compelled to have whatever your substance of choice is at whatever cost.

Now, if you always have one of these substances, whether it's a glass of wine every night or caffeine every day, you don't notice what it's doing to you. That's because it's become part of your normal life experience.

The only way to get an idea of what the substance truly does to you is to stop using it. Go through withdrawal symptoms and then notice the difference. The discomfort at the beginning is nothing compared to how good you feel when you've given it up. Trust me on this.

I became nicotine-free about 20 years ago. Although on rare occasions I still want a cigarette, I resist the urge. I know my first wouldn't be my last.

And I love breathing more easily, tasting the deliciousness of food and not stinking like an old ashtray. Plus, I'm reducing my risks of heart disease, cancer and other goodies which come with this addiction.

I kept trying to give up smoking because I knew it wasn't good for me. But I didn't really want to due to my addicted desire for nicotine. Then, a routine blood test showed I had far too many red blood cells; my blood was dangerously 'sticky'. My arteries were being clogged up, which made me a high risk for heart attack.

My specialist arranged for me to have medical tests, but he was pretty sure my condition was down to smoking. I walked out of his office and threw my cigarette pack away.

On the way home, I bought 24-hour nicotine patches to wean me off. Although it was very difficult to abstain from smoking nicotine at first, I've never smoked since.

It took 20 months for my red blood cells to come within

the normal range, even after I stopped smoking. And, all these years later, my lung age is 10 years older than my real age. Not good!

That's what my addiction did to me. Even so, plenty of people would have continued smoking. Remember, I didn't want to stop. But that blood test result was my wakeup call and I chose a pro-life behaviour instead of an anti-life behaviour.

I made numerous acts of willpower to create a new smokeless habit. I had to make that choice and that action again and again and again until my new learned behaviour was established.

I'm no hero. It was tough at times, but you just have to hack your way through it.

I hope something in my story will trigger a wake-up call moment for you, whatever your substance of choice.

6

DIET

6

DIET

First, a cautionary tale...

It's likely your appetite for food has gone and you're eating too little or nothing at all. Both are good ways to starve yourself to death. Alternatively, food seems to call you all the time and you're eating far too much, gorging yourself to death.

The anti-life depression gremlins don't mind which way you do it. They love them both!

If you're bingeing and gorging yourself, you feel bad. You feel shame. The anti-life gremlins just love that too. They just love you making yourself physically sick in a useless attempt to feel better.

When I've not been able to stop eating, I've stuffed myself with sweets and junk food. A recipe for sugar highs and crashes that made me feel even more unstable and worse.

Then I'd want more sugar to make me feel better. And, as my weight grew, I felt even worse about myself. Shame and more shame. Amazing how those anti-life gremlins entice you to eat rubbish, isn't it?

That's a definite no-win vicious cycle.

At other times when I've been depressed, my appetite would go completely. I felt physically sick when a plate of food was put in front of me. I lost weight wonderfully but felt even worse than before due to lack of nutrition.

In an exceptionally bad bout of no appetite, I woke at 5am one morning and went down to the kitchen for water. It was summer and my south facing garden was flooded with sunlight.

As I opened the door to the kitchen, my eyes were assaulted by beams of sunlight shafting in through the glass back door. It was like an epic movie swooshing the scene with the healing power of light; it flooded me too.

In that moment, a voice in my head said, 'I've been fighting for you.' My body immediately lurched into huge sobs and I realised I had been trying to commit suicide through starvation.

I made myself a huge egg salad there and then, but my jaws wouldn't move. I couldn't get the food into my mouth.

So, I grabbed my nose and pinched my nostrils together so my mouth had to open for air. I shoved some food into it. And, by pushing my chin up and my nose down with my hands, I first forced my teeth to bite on and chew the food. A very purposeful swallow followed.

Within a few minutes, I was able to chew and swallow on my own.

It was like I'd suddenly remembered I wanted to live, and re-connected with my pro-life energy. And I wanted not just to live but to bounce back fully engaged with my Passion.

Breaking the no-eating/over-eating pattern

If you are eating too much, too little, or nothing, eat something small and nourishing on the hour. This fuels your body healthily. It also keeps your blood sugars level. A drop in blood sugars through not eating results in symptoms which mimic anxiety and panic attacks. You can feel very wobbly indeed.

If you're at work or outside the house, take the following, or similar, in a lunch box or plastic bag and eat one an hour:

- A cube of cheese and a wholegrain crisp-bread

- A banana

- A palm full of nuts

- Half a meat or cheese sandwich

- A portion of raw cut up vegetables

- A portion of fruit

- A protein milk shake powder

- A portion of dried fruit

- Peanut butter on a whole-grain rice cake

- A palm full of mixed seeds

Write down some of your own 'small snack' ideas in the margin while you're thinking about them. And, in the evening, just have a tea plate sized meal rather than a normal dinner plate full.

For starvers and over-eaters, the hourly 'small snack' system retrains your appetite in a non-aggressive way. If you blip, be gentle with yourself. It's only a blip and you can put your new eating system back into place as soon as you can.

The pivotal role of H_2O

85% of your body is water. On an average day your body will lose about 2.5 litres. This happens through your lungs, as water vapour; through the skin, as perspiration; and through your kidneys as urine.

If you don't replace that water, dehydration makes you feel anxious, weak and faint. You'll be irritable, lose concentration and find it difficult to think clearly. You'll also feel tired and negative. On top of depression, this is not a good look!

SIP WATER CONSTANTLY THROUGHOUT THE DAY

Sipping 2 to 2.5 litres of water a day should do it. Remember, if you feel thirsty it's too late. You're already dehydrated. The goal is never to feel thirsty by constantly filling up your reservoir with sipping

Carbohydrates

Carbohydrates help healthy brain function and mood; they fill you for longer by creating sustainable energy. None or not enough results in low energy, but...

Avoid carbohydrates that your body absorbs quickly and cause a sugar high, as I talked about in Chapter 5. Instead, eat the carbohydrates your body slowly absorbs, both for energy and to help recovery. These include wholegrain products, fruit, vegetables and legumes like beans, peas and lentils.

Some easy to make, good carbohydrate meals are:

- Jacket potato with chicken mayo salad and green beans. Eat the potato skin for loads of vitamins.

- Jacket potato with cheese and/or baked beans. Ditto re skin.

- Wholegrain muesli with sliced fruit and yoghurt

- Whole grain porridge with a sprinkle of nuts

- Scrambled or poached eggs and/or beans on whole grain toast

- A pile of cooked, mixed fresh or frozen vegetables with a dollop of mayonnaise

- Grilled sardines on whole grain toast with grilled tomato halves

- Make a nourishing soup from two chicken/beef stock cubes, diced fresh or frozen mixed vegetables, ready-to-cook lentils, and seasoning (anything from chilli or paprika to marmite or soy sauce)

- Baked beans with a few drops of chilli or hot pepper sauce, with baked yam and fresh or frozen peas

Experiment with a mix and match of any of the above and jot down some of your own ideas in the margin.

5 a day

Eat at least five portions of fruit and vegetables a day. They're full of vitamins and micro-nutrients to keep us healthy in our body, feelings, mind and ooomph. Definitely bounce back fuel.

Have more vegetables than fruit; vegetables generally contain less sugar than fruit. My blood sugars shot up to diabetic level when I was over-dosing on fruit a few years ago. You have been warned!

Steam or cook all vegetables lightly in a small amount of pre-boiled water and eat them still crisp. If you eat them soft and soggy most of the vitamins will have leached into the water. Save vegetable cooking water as a base for easy soups.

And why not eat raw vegetables as snacks rather than junk food like crisps and confectionary? Here are some ideas:

- Vegetable sticks on their own, or to dip into hummus, peanut butter or cream cheese

- Celery sticks filled with any of the above

- Olives, having been rolled in kitchen paper to remove excess oil

- Small chunks of cauliflower sprinkled with chilli powder or spread thinly with mayonnaise or salad cream

- Big chunk of cucumber sliced lengthwise into sticks, with a dip or sprinkled with crushed nuts or sunflower seeds

- Sections of a crispy small white cabbage

Experiment with a mix and match of the above and, of course, jot your own vegetable snack ideas in the margin.

Protein

You need protein to keep your skin, organs, muscles and immune system healthy. It also influences positive mood which is another bounce back benefit.

Protein includes foods like meat, fish, eggs, cheese, nuts, beans, and lentils. You can also find protein in meat substitutes like vegetable protein, beans and soya products.

All of the easy meals and snacks I've suggested previously have included some of the above. While we'd all love a roast, my favourite – baked beans – is just as delicious in its own way. And scrambled or poached eggs on wholegrain toast with fruity sauce? I love that meal.

Omega 3

People who don't regularly eat oily fish, which is high in Omega-3 fatty acids, have been found more likely to suffer depression than those who do. So, include in your diet three times a week, oily fish such as salmon, trout, sardines, mackerel and fresh tuna. Other than tuna, which loses Omega 3 by being canned, your oily fish can be fresh, frozen or canned.

Other good food sources for Omega-3 include flaxseed, nuts, dark leafy vegetables, avocados and tofu.

Here are some easy to make meal ideas:

- Sardine and tomato sandwich with wholegrain bread.

- Mackerel in tomato sauce with cooked fresh or frozen diced vegetables.

- Avocado with French dressing.

- Fresh or drained canned salmon mashed up with a small diced onion or spring onions and mayonnaise, salad cream or tomato sauce with salad or in a wholegrain sandwich.

- Sprinkle nuts and/or seeds on a salad or cooked mixed vegetables

As always, jot down your own ideas in the margin.

Vitamin D3

There's some suggestion that Vitamin D3 deficiency is also associated with depression.

We produce this vitamin under the skin in reaction to summer sunlight. Vitamin D is also found in a small number of foods such as:

- oily fish

- eggs

- fortified fat spreads

- fortified breakfast cereals

You can, of course, also buy Vitamin D3 as a supplement as you can other vitamins.

B-Complex vitamins

These are the whole range of B vitamins essential for mental and emotional well-being. You can find them in spinach, broccoli, meat, fish, poultry, whole grains, vegetables, bananas, eggs and dary produce.

You might have noticed that several foods here have also been listed in other categories. So, use suggestions I've made previously as well as the above. Because you'll help your recovery when you

EAT A WIDE VARIETY OF FOODS

The more varied your diet the more likely you will get all the nutrients you need. This is true whether you're on the hourly 'small snacks' system, regaining your appetite or back to your normal eating. Eating the colours of the rainbow in vegetables will also help.

If money is tight

Buy super-market specials and their budget range vegetables. Frozen vegetables can be cheaper and better than fresh, which lose vitamins depending on how not-fresh they are!

Buy own brand, good value, fresh fruits, vegetables and foods in your local supermarket. The fruit and vegetables might look a little misshapen but, hey, that's how many of them look when grown naturally.

Be adventurous with your meals. In a time of financial crisis and in danger of house repossession, I fed our then family of four on things like:

- Vegetable stews spiced up with the goodness of Marmite, plus sometimes chilli powder or hot pepper sauce, accompanied by cheese and wholegrain bread.

- Tinned mackerel flaked into brown rice with chopped boiled egg and colourful diced vegetables, followed by stewed fruit and custard.

- Chunky cut vegetables with yummy fried onion mixed in plus baked sweet potatoes, followed by gently simmered pears (or 'on offer' fruit of the day) sprinkled with cinnamon powder.

I could also do a million things with minced meat. Meat balls, meat loaf, spag bol, stuffed cabbage and lasagne, for example. Mixed with other ingredients like chopped onion, rice, egg and maize (or flour) plus seasoning of your choice, then rolled into balls and simmered in stock, a little minced meat goes a long way.

We were never healthier.

In conclusion

This is a short and by no means complete guide to a diet which can help you bounce back from depression. So, when you're ready, you could surf the internet for more ideas.

Remember the old saying, 'garbage in, garbage out'? The stuff we eat is involved in not only recovering from depression but keeping ourselves healthy beyond depression too.

7

THERAPY

7

THERAPY

What is therapy?

Dictionaries say therapy is a treatment intended to cure or alleviate an illness or injury, whether physical or mental.

Here's my definition of therapy in relation to depression and other psychological, mental and emotional issues.

'Therapy' is a process offered to you by another human being with the knowledge, skills and, hopefully, wisdom to help you help yourself to:

- Recover from whatever it is that distresses you and learn lessons the experience offers you

- If needed, find a resolution to some situation or difficulty which is right for you

- Learn more about who you really are rather than who you were trained to be

- Leave the therapy with more self-awareness and some take-away skills to help yourself on your own

- Get a clear idea of what moving forward looks like for you and develop some resources and abilities to get you there

To have therapy or not?

My question is, if you can get some therapy, why not?

Depression is an experience which affects your feelings, body, mind and your oomph, whatever you believe your oomph to be. My experience is working therapeutically with depression from a whole person perspective, with body, feelings, mind and oomph, speeds up recovery. It enables you to bounce back far sooner than you would imagine.

So, if you can afford it, why not work with a therapist who can help you recover from depression? A therapist who can also help you use depression as a personal growth opportunity.

If you can't afford it, please ask your GP for a counselling referral. Unfortunately, there's usually a long delay for counsellors provided by your GP or the NHS.

But, by using this book you'll already be doing a lot on your own to help you recover. You can ask a trusted and empathetic family member or friend to be your 'accountability buddy'. Every two to three days tell them what you're doing and going to do from this book as a next step.

They then gently encourage you and check you're on track, providing encouraging support if you blip. Be gentle with yourself if you do. This is not about getting recovery right or wrong. It's about you being supported and encouraged to find your own way through recovery.

Research has found that having an accountability buddy helps you to achieve what you want faster and more easily than by doing it on your own. So, who could be your accountability buddy?

Which therapy?

There are hundreds of different therapies. So, I'm not going to confuse you with lists and definitions. You can always google 'psychotherapy' if you want to know more.

The next section will help you find a therapist who is right for you. By 'therapist' I mean someone who has trained to be a counsellor or psychotherapist.

How to choose a therapist – recommendations and registers

If you know someone who's been in therapy, ask them how they got on and, if good, ask for the therapist's contact details. Your GP or other health professionals might be able to recommend particular therapists too.

That doesn't mean a recommended therapist is the right one for you. Or that all therapists are equally effective. More of that later.

You can search for therapists in your area through professional organisations that monitor their members and insist on codes of ethics and practice. They also have robust complaint procedures if needed.

In this respect, I highly recommend the British Association for Counselling and Psychotherapy www.bacp.co.uk

You will notice that some therapists are accredited and/or registered. These are therapists who have gone through extra hoops to demonstrate their professionalism and skills.

That doesn't necessarily mean they are the right therapist for you. More about that later.

What to ask a prospective therapist

Ask as many questions as you like in your first phone call to a therapist. You are the customer. If the therapist doesn't want to answer your questions, they're not the right therapist for you.

If the therapist says you have to/must/should come to an initial session to have your questions answered, they're also not the right therapist for you.

You'll be paying a therapist for their services. So, interview them.

What you're looking for is no BS. That means honest replies, including declining to reply to any question with their reasons for doing so. Here are your basic interview questions.

1. What are your qualifications and how long have you been a therapist?

2. Which professional organisation do you belong to and are you accredited? (Accredited means they have to meet certain criteria, like so many hours of study per year and regular supervision.)

   You can now choose a counsellor or psychotherapist in the UK belonging to a register approved by the Professional Standards Authority for Health and Social Care. Other registers do not have this stamp of approval.

3. Ask them, 'Are you on a register approved by the Professional Standards Authority for Health and Social Care?' This is another sign of professionalism but still doesn't mean this therapist is right for you.

4. How often do you have professional supervision? (It should be at least monthly for about 1.5 hours).

5. What experience do you have working with depressed people?

6. Have you ever been depressed yourself? (I think it's essential your therapist has been depressed. People who haven't been depressed themselves will not

understand your experience in a million years. They can imagine it and empathise but they just won't get it).

7. What kind of therapy do you do, and why do you think this would be effective for me?

8. What are your fees?

Now, here's a very important question to ask yourself during your telephone conversation with a therapist.

Do I feel comfortable with this person?

The relationship between you and your therapist is crucial as to whether your therapy is successful or not. So, choose someone who you feel comfortable talking to.

An initial face-to-face appointment is a further opportunity to see whether you're absolutely at ease with them and where they work. Some therapists, like me, have a consulting room in their own home. Others will work in organisations and offices. Where do you feel most comfortable?

Another cautionary tale

I once wanted a therapist to help me get to grips with a challenging relationship. I did my research and chose five therapists in my area with the appropriate professional qualifications and credibility.

I interviewed them for the 'job' in my first phone call with a standardised spiel. To each of them I said, 'Hi, I'm Sharon Eden, a shit-hot psychotherapist who's looking for a shit-hot psychotherapist who can challenge me.'

I admit that was challenging but I wanted a really good therapist who could and would challenge me. I can fool myself like anyone else. And if they couldn't face a challenge themselves then they wouldn't be able to do it for me.

The first therapist was totally put off by what I said. Not the right therapist for me.

The second therapist said I couldn't properly assess if she was the right therapist for me without coming to an initial assessment. She was wrong. You can tell whether a therapist is right for you within minutes of talking on the telephone.

The third therapist didn't return my call... ever.

The fourth therapist put up a valiant response but I could hear the hesitancy in his voice. Not the right therapist for me.

By now I was wondering whether I would ever find a therapist who fitted with me. So, I phoned the fifth and final therapist on my list without much hope.

When I'd said my standard spiel, I heard the most delicious giggle on the other end of the line. 'Oh,' she said, 'I'm not sure I'm up to you!' I replied, 'When can I have an appointment to see you?'

This therapist was absolutely honest and open with me. She was being herself rather than how she thought a therapist should be. She was also confident in herself and most likely to provide me with the challenge I needed. It turned out that I was right!

DON'T SETTLE FOR THE FIRST THERAPIST YOU CALL.

Contact several and compare them. Ask your questions and persevere until you find one right for you.

Therapists to avoid at all costs

Therapists who say they can cure or heal you

Healing will come from within you. Plus, depression is not a condition to be cured. It's to be embraced, leaned in to and, in recovery, to be tapped for the personal development which lies in its shadows. Depression is a growth opportunity.

Therapists who want to trawl through your life to find the reasons you're depressed

When you're depressed, the last thing you need is to bring up past traumatising or painful events. You haven't got the resources to deal with them and they might trigger even deeper depression and anxieties.

The first job at the beginning of therapy is to build some solid foundations for you to stand on. Some will be internal, like seeing things as they are rather than through the negative mist of your depression. Others might well be external, like getting advice from the Citizen's Advice Bureau on finances, for example, or confiding things to a trusted friend.

With some foundations in place, you can then move forward to explore old events, memories of which have been triggered by current events... if that's useful for you.

Sometimes it is and sometimes it's only useful as background information. Like, 'Oh now I get it. Uncle George was critical of and horrible to me. That's part of how I came to be so upset and get so upset now if it seems like I'm being criticised.'

What's very useful is to deal with the here and now and moving forward. That might include working with parts of your personality stuck in the past. But, generally, you don't have to trawl methodically through all of your past for therapy to help you. Nor do you have to re-experience all your emotions from the past.

WHEN YOU'RE DEPRESSED, HAVE TRAUMA IN YOUR PAST AND A THERAPIST WANTS TO TAKE YOU BACK INTO YOUR TRAUMA, SAY NO, IF YOU CAN, OR LEAVE IMMEDIATELY.

Taking you back into your trauma will only re-traumatise you and reinforce all the physical, mental and emotional feelings you had then. The danger is of you feeling all of that again and making your depression even worse.

Avoid depression therapy groups like the plague

Because you'll become part of a depression party. You'll just reinforce how awful you feel and how shit the world seems.

Depression is contagious. It can spread like flu. So, no sooner do you start feeling better than you get re-infected by somebody else in the group.

You might be offered a depression therapy group by the NHS or a charity as it's cheaper than individual therapy. If you decide to join one, be active in not joining in discussions about how awful depression is or reinforcing depressed symptoms.

Instead, ask the group leader for techniques to help navigate your darkness. Also, ask the group leader to explore what everyone's strengths are and how these might help recovery. Asking for a constructive approach in the group will better resource you and help build those foundations I mentioned earlier.

Avoid other depressed people like the plague

Just talking on the phone with another depressed person can make you feel even more depressed. Politely say no to them. For example, 'I'm unable to talk with you right now. I'll get back in touch when I'm feeling better.'

I remember being with a friend who started telling me several bad luck stories when I was depressed. They triggered me into even greater fear and anxiety. Thankfully, I was able to say, 'Please only talk about good things.' And she did.

Only speak and be with positive people who can reassure you that you will recover, even when you feel you won't. Plus, positive people's good vibrations will rub off on you. Not to begin with, maybe. Yet, keep on meeting them, being with them, talking with them. And, in time, the magic works.

GOOD VIBRATIONS ARE CONTAGIOUS TOO!

8

OBSTACLES TO RECOVERY

8

OBSTACLES TO RECOVERY

There are many reasons why people struggle in their recovery journey. It's unlikely you'll experience all the obstacles listed below. Choose the ones you recognise and work with them one at a time, using the suggested technique.

This will help greatly lessen the impact of the ones that affect you, at the very least. At the very best, the technique could get rid of those obstacles altogether.

Negative, dark thoughts and obsessive thinking

Dark or negative thoughts are often fuelled by the way the media reports news in the papers, through TV, radio, and online. It's mainly about very depressing stuff: war, terrorism, crimes, child abuse, political scandals and hard luck stories.

So avoid news of any kind for the moment. It will only make your thoughts and feelings worse. These range from 'I'm a pile of poo' to thoughts of killing yourself, and everything in between like shame, helplessness, hopelessness and self-hatred.

How those anti-life gremlin energies just love to torment you. They expect you to either go under or fight them. If you go under, they do a celebration dance. If you fight them, they do a celebration dance. In either case, they suck out your energy.

Instead, embrace those anti-life gremlins by saying in a kind of hammed up way, 'Thank you so much for telling me that. But, right now I'm *reading Sharon's book.*' Replace the action with whatever it is you're doing as you talk, such as walking down the road, having a cup of tea or brushing your hair.

Why?

Acknowledging, rather than fighting, the dark thoughts makes your anti-life gremlins relax and deflate with an 'Oooooh, s/he really heard me!' Because all they really want is for you to acknowledge that you've registered their message.

Particularly good for obsessive thinking is clapping hands furiously for a minute or pinching the inside of your thigh at the top of your leg so it hurts. These techniques interrupt your pattern of repetitive thinking brilliantly. Repeat as needed… usually often to begin with.

Disturbed sleep

Are you unable to get to sleep and/or find yourself frequently waking up in the night? Being awake in the middle of the night when it's dark and everybody else is sleeping is pants. So, here are some tips. Download more Sleeping Tips from the Resource page of my website www.bouncebackuk.com

- Make sure your bedroom is comfortably cool, well ventilated and absolutely pitch black at night. The darkness signals to our brain it's time to sleep.

- Remove all technology from your bedroom. We can be disturbed by emissions we don't even register, especially from ipads and tablets.

- Start winding down 90 minutes before bed-time, including switching off TV, computers and tablets. Just as with children, a period of down-time leading to bed-time can encourage sleep.

- Keep doing these things even if they don't make a difference at first. Remember, you are building a new habit. Give it time.

Anxiety

Anxiety is also the pits. Here are some techniques:

- Breathe in and out of a paper bag tightly sealed round your mouth with one hand until you calm.

- Breathe in the following sequence

  Breathe in through your nose for the count of 1, 2, and 3

  Breathe out noisily through your mouth for the count of 1, 2, 3, and 4.

  Hold your breath for the count of 1, 2, and 3.

  Repeat twice more.

Both techniques change the ratio of blood gases in your brain to trigger the 'relax' part of your nervous system, which calms you down.

Use the breathing sequence for as long as you can before you gasp for air and this will trigger your sleep mechanism. Even if you have to do it more than once in the night, this will help you get more sleep.

Unless you're a Martian, these techniques work by co-operating with how your body works normally. You might have to repeat them every five minutes to begin with, but persevere. You're re-training your nervous system.

Because anxiety feels as if you're in a threatening situation, even if you're not, building in safety seems to alleviate it. Research suggests that seeing pictures of someone else being loved and cared for is an antidote to anxiety. So cut out pictures of scenes like this from magazines that can be ready to use when you need them.

Suicidal thoughts?

Get help: GP, out of hours doctor or A & E. Phoning the Samaritans can support you too: 08457 90 90 90 for the UK. Or find your nearest branch by going to www.samaritans.org.uk/branches

I can't stop you killing yourself if you actually decide to go ahead. What I do know is that you will be missed. And you will miss out on a heck of a lot to come in your life.

Re-read the list in Chapter 1 (Wanting to kill yourself) of all the wonderful things I would never have known if I had killed myself. Some of them could be yours too.

Fear of change

Depression often happens in times of change, usually involving the loss of something or someone. It's a very understandable reaction.

None of us likes change, but it's a fact of life. The bottom line is, do you want depression in your life or do you want to feel more alive? If you want to feel more alive, learn how to live with change.

Sure, it's scary. You have to face whatever the change is and come to terms with it. But I promise you, anything but *anything* worth doing triggers fear because you'll be going outside of your same-old-same-old comfort zone.

Stay as you are in depression or start facing reality, whatever it is. Acknowledging even a small bit of 'what is' can begin to move you forward and into recovery bounce back.

Overwhelm and 'I can't'

This is the feeling that you have too much to cope with in your life. Tell yourself, 'I can't cope' and you turn yourself into a victim. Tell yourself instead, 'I won't cope' and notice how different you feel.

You turn yourself into someone who *has* the power to cope and chooses not to use it at the moment; a person who has willpower.

It's a subtle difference which puts you in charge. It gives you the option to cope later.

One way to reconnect with your coping ability is to think how you could eat an elephant? Bit by bit, of course. So, break down the thing you're choosing not to cope with into bite size pieces. Start nibbling!

Procrastination

Are you unable to make up your mind, even about very simple things like which sort of sandwich to eat for lunch?

That's because it's difficult to make decisions when you're depressed. Negative thinking, confusion and stress/anxiety just knock out your ability to do so. So, if possible, avoid making any important and life-changing decisions when you're depressed.

Unfortunately, sometimes depression comes hand in hand with life-changing situations where decisions are needed. If that's you, friends and family are usually too biased and emotionally involved to give you clear advice. So, get some very solid and unbiased advice from a professional in whatever area you have to make a decision.

IN ALL OTHER AND EVERY DAY MATTERS, JUST CHOOSE!

Go on. Just make a decision, any decision. In the big scheme of things it doesn't matter what sandwich you have for lunch. Plus, through the action of choosing, you exercise and build the muscles of your will power. This is a powerful way to fox the anti-life gremlins and encourage your bounce back.

Excuses for not getting better

Please be gentle with yourself about this one. I know you want to get better. It's just that a part of you doesn't. That's the part of you that is scared about facing whatever reality you need to face.

It tells you things like 'If you get better you'll have to go back to that job you hate.' Or 'If s/he sees how ill I am they will/won't… ' Write on the dotted line something you're scared someone will do or won't do. Or, 'As long as I'm depressed, I'll get looked after', or 'I won't have to do... ' Write in here something you don't want to do.

Your anti-life gremlin energy tells you it's risky to face whatever reality you need to face. You bet it is. Life *can* be risky.

So, what are you going to do? Hide your head in the sand for the entire rest of your life... like forever?

You might not know how things are going to turn out. But, is depression going to make life any safer or easier for you? I don't think so.

So grab yourself by your balls, whether real or metaphorical, and do the thing that's scaring you most, whatever it is.

It's never as awful as your anti-life gremlins have made you imagine.You'll feel so much better mentally, emotionally and psychologically when you've faced it. And you'll feel immense relief as the tension of the fear you've been carrying releases.

Guilt, shame and blame

These are big guns!

Guilt

Feeling guilt means 'I did something bad'. That might or might not be true.

I once worked with a man who felt guilty about divorcing his ex-wife as his life had moved on and hers had not. He blamed himself for her current misery.

When I started to challenge his version of reality, he recognised he had made some choices and so had his ex-wife. It was not that he had *made* her miserable. At some level, she was making a choice to be miserable by not facing up to her reality and moving on with life.

However, if you've actually done something wrong according to your moral code, it's time for action.

A wise teacher once told me that if you've made a mess and can go back and clear it up, do so. Then move on. If you've made a mess and there's no way you can go back and clear it up, just move on.

Shame

Feeling shame means, 'I *am* bad'. This is never true even if you've done bad things. Who you are at essence is a loving and humane human being, even if you don't feel that right now.

Your 'I am bad' messages might come as thoughts of 'I'm not good enough' or 'I don't deserve good things/love/success' or 'No-one will ever love me'. Or something else like that.

These messages or beliefs are learned during childhood. Like not being born the 'right' gender baby for a parent or being compared unfavourably with someone else. Like being treated so badly that you come to the conclusion 'I *must* be bad because, if I was good, this (painful thing) wouldn't be happening to me'.

One way to start turning this round is to start telling yourself, 'I am enough'. Repeat at every opportunity, 'I am enough' because you most certainly are.

Blame

Blaming others including the system, the world or God is a cop out. It only turns you into a victim. At the same time, blaming yourself is erroneously beating yourself up big-time.

There's a big difference between blaming and taking responsibility for what you've done if you have, indeed, done anything wrong at all. If you have done something wrong, re-read the suggestion on how to deal with guilt.

So...

I now give you permission (or give yourself permission) to dump your guilt, shame and blame. Throw them all like big, steaming clumps of manure way out into the Universe. Let them disappear as tiny dots into infinity.

Repeat as necessary.

Habit

You can be so used to being depressed that it turns into a habit and a way of being. Depression becomes your identity. Better the devil you know than the one you don't.

If you've been depressed before, you might also interpret any low mood or emotional difficulty as slipping into depression. You're not. But if you think you are, guess what happens?

One technique for creating new behaviours is to say and think a phrase like, 'Right now I am absolutely content'. Use whatever quality of being you feel lacking in your life, for example, loved, confident, fearless, courageous or determined. This technique re-programmes your brain so repeat, repeat and repeat until you do, indeed, feel as you wish.

Remember learning to drive a car or a bicycle? At first you have to concentrate on how to do it. Then, through repeating 'how to do it' actions again and again, you start driving automatically without thinking.

It's the same when you're putting in place new ways of behaving, thinking and feeling. Keep repeating the 'how to do it' actions. In this case the action, use of willpower, is the sentence about the quality you want in your life. In about 21 to 26 days, prepare to be surprised and delighted by having that behaviour become automatic for you too.

That technique is also a good way to start edging out your depression identity, if you have one.

Suicidal thoughts

I can't stop you killing yourself if you decide to do it. What I know is that you'll both be missed and miss out on a whole lot of life to come.

Re-read the section on wanting to kill yourself in Chapter 1, particularly my list of wonderful things I would never have known if I'd committed suicide. Some of them could be your wonderful things too.

9

BOUNCE BACK WITH PRO-LIFE ENERGIES

9

BOUNCE BACK WITH
PRO-LIFE ENERGIES

I've written about the anti-life energies, the gremlins. Now it's time to talk more about pro-life energies.

As mentioned earlier, Passion is the #1 energy to help you bounce back from depression. It's your oomph, whatever you believe your oomph to be. And it can be channelled in many different ways. Here are some:

Enlisting help from non-depressed you

You might feel overwhelmed and over-run by your depression and believe that's all you are. But it's not.

We're made up of many different personality 'parts'. And the part of you that's depressed has taken the major role in your life for now. The part of you that isn't depressed has been pushed aside. But it's still there, even if you don't feel it.

I once worked with a woman who was suicidal and suffering from some highly anxiety-provoking thoughts.

99

She didn't look at me when we were speaking, and had difficulty stringing two sentences together. I asked her if I could speak to the part of her who was not depressed.

Immediately, she changed. More colour came into her skin. She was able to look at me and speak more clearly. She sat upright and was far more alert.

By realising she could connect to her not-depressed part, she was able to enlist it to help her depressed part in recovery. For example, she could use it to remind herself her pro-life energies were still there. By so doing, she was able to begin negating those anxiety provoking thoughts.

You can do the same.

A quick way to connect with not-depressed you is to change your body position. Sit up with your spine straight and your head straight. Put both feet squarely on the ground before you.

Give that a go now and notice the difference in how you feel. Then stand up with this straight spine posture and walk around a little. Notice the difference here too.

With your body in this posture, practise behaving as if you aren't depressed you, even for a few minutes at a time. This re-connects you with your pro-life energies as well as exercising and strengthening connective muscle to them.

This technique is also known as 'fake it until you make it'. What you imagine you can become. So, practise, practise, practise.

Love

Love might be about the last thing you want to think about if you're in a negative place. Yet I remember how my children's love gave me a smidgeon of comfort in some of my dark hours.

Love is a 100% pro-life energy. It can melt the hardest and most mean person if they open up to it. So, just think what it could do for you.

What made you feel loved as a child? Heinz tomato soup, toasted crumpets drenched with melting butter, egg and cress sandwiches? You can tell my thing was food! What was yours?

Cuddling your pet? Running until you and the wind were one? Losing yourself in a special book? Being with your Nan? A neighbour's tea and biscuits?

I remember being five and washing my hands with Lifebuoy soap at our next door neighbour's house before teatime. I felt loved and cared for in their home. And I always associate the safety and kindness they gave me with the smell and sudsy feel of that soap.

Whatever your love thing is or memory was, give it to yourself in reality or imagine having it right now. Your mind doesn't know the difference between something really happening and it happening in your imagination. So, either way, you're onto a winner.

Purpose

Having a sense of purpose, what you're here to do in the world, gives life meaning. Depression often means you feel you've lost your purpose or weren't connected with it in the first place.

The good news is that it's not really lost. At some point your purpose went underground in the face of anti-life gremlin attacking energy, internal or external.

'Don't be silly!' You'll never earn a living doing that.' 'You can't do that!'

Being, let's say, artistic but following someone's advice to dump that in favour of a 'proper' job. That could be following in a parent's footsteps as the sensible thing to do or never being encouraged to discover what you really want to do.

So you wisely hid your purpose, perhaps before you even knew what it was, to keep it safe from the gremlins and other people. All that's happened, for now, is you've forgotten where you put it.

So, let this be your purpose for now:

'My purpose, right now, is to embrace and recover from depression.' Write those words on a big piece of paper in large letters to stick on your fridge. Read and say out loud at least three times every day.

Humour

Humour is nature's anti-depressant and pain reliever. It's also an expression of your Passion designed to be an excellent and natural coping mechanism. It's helped people in concentration camps, wars and deprivations of all kinds to cope with their reality. So, think what it could do for you.

Watch DVDs of your favourite comedians and humorous shows. Even if you don't feel able to laugh, the humour works to stimulate your pro-life energies.

Smile 20 times all in one go. Even if you don't feel smiley, working on those smile muscles sends pro-life messages to your brain. Repeat daily until your smiling becomes natural and real. Remember how acting 'as if' helps recovery?

Prayer

You might follow a religion which includes prayer in its practice. But you don't need to in order to pray.

I cover all bases by starting my prayers with 'God, Goddess, Great Spirit, Universe and all the Positive Forces in the Universe... '

Or, you could direct your prayer to your Higher Self, the Divine, Yoda or the earth beneath your feet. Whatever symbolises universal pro-life energy for you.

If you're going to ask for something, ask for what you want more of rather than what you don't want. 'I want peace, please' is far more effective than 'I don't want anxiety' as your mind will focus on whatever you tell it to. And peace rather than anxiety is the way to go.

My prayers start with gratitude. I say the 'God, Goddess... ' section and then, usually, 'Thank you for all the riches and abundance in my life.'

Being grateful for positive things helps you recognise where you already have them. And you do have them, however negative you feel. The sun glinting on a glass bottle in a gutter was my only positive thing once on a dark day. How grateful I was to experience the light in my dark.

Express gratitude for whatever good thing/s you have in your life today, however tiny it/they might feel. Whatever we focus on grows. So, make sure you focus on the good stuff to get those pro-life energies active.

That's my way of praying. A song, poem or painting can be prayer. Walking with an open heart can also be a prayer. Cooking a meal can be a prayer.

Pray in whatever way works for you.

Gratitude

While I'm talking about gratitude, write down five things for which you're grateful before you go to bed every night.

One thing to be grateful for could be that you got out of bed this morning or managed to brush your teeth. One might be a picture you saw, a bird you heard singing or a friend's telephone call. Write down anything, but anything for which you're glad.

Make that pro-life practice the very last thing you think about and do before bedtime every night. In time, this will help improve the quality of your sleep.

Dancing

Here are the benefits of dancing...

- Dancing oxygenates your body. This is important when, in stress or depression, you breathe shallowly, so you don't take in enough oxygen, the pro-life elixir for aliveness. No wonder you feel endlessly tired with depression.

- Dancing is physical exercise which, apart from helping your body, can make you tired in the kind of way that encourages sleep. So dance several times a day.

- Dancing stimulates your oomph and the feel-good chemicals in your brain. These are more pro-life energies which will lift your mood.

Put on a CD or DVD of energetic and upbeat music with positive lyrics. Even if you don't feel like it, start letting your body move however it wants to with the beat of the music. Another little act of willpower which, in a few moments, enables your body to relax and go-go-go.

Sometimes I close my eyes and let my body rip, cavorting in ways I just wouldn't in public. Sheer heaven.

Songs

I've also had particular emblem songs to help me bounce back from depression. In a particularly severe depression, I had 'The Wind Beneath my Wings' by Bette Midler. At another time, my song was 'Hero' by Mariah Carey.

You can play a video of each song on the Resource page of my website www.bouncebackuk.com

These songs are pro-life energies which still nourish my heart, mind, guts and Soul. What would be your emblem song right now?

Repetitive physical activity

Apart from dancing, mentioned earlier, there's exercising at the gym, going for very brisk walks every day, jogging and running up and down stairs, for example. Any energetic and repetitive physical activity will boost 'feel good' chemicals in your brain and pro-life energies.

I prefer dancing at home because I can absolutely let rip on any inhibitions, get into the zone and go for it 100%. If that's not for you, get some daily exercise like at least 15 minutes brisk walk round the streets or a local park. Every little bit of repetitive physical activity will help you bounce back from depression.

Inspirational quotations

This is another of my favourite ways to connect with my Passion and pro-life energies. Inspirational quotations nourish your body, feelings, mind and ooomph.

Here are some I just found through googling 'Inspirational Quotes':

'Your present circumstances don't determine where you can go; they merely determine where you start.'

Nido Qubein

'Go confidently in the direction of your dreams.
Live the life you have imagined.'

Henry David Thoreau

'Our greatest weakness lies in giving up.
The most certain way to succeed is always
to try just one more time.'

Thomas A. Edison

'If you're going through hell, keep going.'

Winston Churchill

You can also buy books of inspirational quotations. You can actually find one I wrote earlier, *365 Inner Leadership*, by going to www.bounceback.uk/resources

Make a list of your favourite quotations. Keep it near to hand for a quick pro-life energy boost whenever you need one.

Being awake and depressed in the middle of the night is horrible. So, in a suicidal depression, I made three hand-written A4 sheets of my favourite inspirational quotations and saved them for those dark times.

Reading them over and over, even saying them out loud, helped take the edge off my inner torment. Fuelling myself with their pro-life energy helped see me through those nights.

To help you give this a go, there's a list of inspirational quotations at the end of this book, chosen especially for you.

You can also sign up for my free early morning e-mail Bounce Back Prompts. These are one-sentence inspirational messages created with you in mind. Sign up for them at www.bouncebackuk.com

10

THE POWER OF ACTION

10

THE POWER OF ACTION

Action = achievements = lift your mood

'Action is the antidote to despair.'

Joan Baez

'Without Passion, you don't have energy;
without energy, you have nothing.'

Donald Trump

Remember, Passion is your ultimate pro-life energy. It seems to do a disappearing act in depression. However, the secret is by taking action even when you don't feel like it you will unconsciously start connecting with and exercising your Passion muscles.

It doesn't matter what action you take. Just take it!

Set yourself a target, from brushing your teeth or phoning a friend, to a 5-mile run or delivering a presentation, depending on where you are with depression at the time. Write your target down.

When you've achieved it, enjoy ticking it off and that you did, indeed, reach your target. Notice how achievement lifts your mood even for a nano-second, although usually it's a lot more.

If by any chance you blip, be gentle with yourself. You might have set a target which, in reality, was a bit beyond what you could achieve right now. I've certainly done that in the past.

So, set yourself another and more realistic target which stretches you just a little. Remember how you eat that elephant? Bit by bit.

Throughout this book I've asked you to do things. Whenever you do something, however small, it's an achievement. Especially if you feel so unmotivated you could drop off the edge of the earth.

A series of little achievements start to rebuild your identity as an achiever. The more you do, the more you feed yourself with pro-life energy and help lift your mood.

So, women, start by putting on some 'slap.' Men, shave and put on some aftershave. Start looking as you would normally or as near to as possible. Get out of those sloppy clothes and put something on you really like wearing.

Act as if you're in a lifted mood and you'll end up becoming who/what you're pretending to be.

Getting-up and brushing your teeth could be your action achievement of the day. If that's so, well done you. That's a triumph when everything in you wants to hide under the duvet.

Structure

Before you felt depressed, you probably had a structure to your day. I know some of you will still have it if you're going to work or have children to get to school or care for someone else.

If you're off sick or unemployed or retired, get yourself a diary and schedule things in to create structure. Start with your getting-up time: getting up the same time every day encourages your bounce back. So, set your alarm and get up at whatever time you've chosen.

Schedule in two brisk walks a day. Schedule in clearing out one drawer or whatever small task/s you decide on. Remember, action = achievement = lift your mood.

Also schedule in a small treat every day. Make it something you normally enjoy. It might be kicking a ball around in the back garden, doing a small amount of gardening, getting a special magazine or painting your nails. Choose whatever works for you.

Each time you complete one of your scheduled tasks or treats, tick it off energetically as another pro-life triumph.

If you already have a structure in your life, get a diary and schedule in what you're already doing so you can see it in black and white. Having it before your eyes helps you appreciate what you are achieving even though you're depressed.

Structure holds you safely in its boundaries. You know what you're doing and when. It helps create a foundation of action achievements to stand on. These in turn form part of the solid foundations from which you can bounce back from depression and build yourself anew.

And, as your recovery increases, you can turn that small daily treat into an even bigger one!

'Do or do not. There is no try.'

Yoda in *Star Wars*

Anti-life gremlin energy just loves beating you up for what you don't do.

So if you stumble in your action progress and miss doing what you had scheduled to do, be very gentle with yourself. No telling yourself off, please.

Recovery from depression is not linear. It has its highs and lows. Just brush yourself down and start all over again. As the Japanese quotation says, 'Fall down seven times. Get up eight times.'

Focus on what you achieve, however small, even if it is one thing a day. Congratulate yourself on doing it. Tell yourself, 'Well done, me!' This helps build your self-esteem and belief in yourself.

Remember, focus on what you do rather on what you don't do. Action = achievements = lift your mood. And always, but always, reward yourself for doing it. You are a star!

Treat yourself as a delicious lover would

I bet you think that's a big ask.

You're so used to putting yourself down, telling yourself off and generally beating yourself up for not being good enough. And that's even before you got depressed.

So the idea of treating yourself as a delicious lover would runs heavily against the grain. So what? It's time to start challenging those misguided, anti-life gremlin thoughts and behaviours. Remember, what you are is perfect imperfection and you are absolutely enough.

Here are some ways of treating yourself as a delicious lover would...

• Buy or pick yourself colourful flowers. Men can appreciate flowers too.

• Treat yourself to a small carton of your favourite ice-cream.

- Pack a picnic. Even in winter, wrapped up well and with a bin bag to sit on in case of any damp, a picnic can be a special treat.

- Send yourself a card, or letter, writing down what a delicious lover would want to say to you.

- Scatter 'love messages' round your home written on post-its which you'll come across from time to time. I found one today tucked in an old diary. What a lovely surprise!

Show yourself love and compassion

I felt the anti-life gremlins start a protest march when I wrote that. Love and compassion, for heaven's sake? Whoever heard of such a thing?

You might never have been taught to give yourself love and compassion. Have a go at the following exercise using your imagination. You can also download the pdf 'Show Yourself Love and Compassion' from the resources page of my website www.bouncebackuk.com

People imagine in different ways. For example, I never get 'pictures' but just sense what I'm being asked to imagine. Whatever way you imagine is absolutely OK.

Here goes...

Choose a day and time to do this when you are feeling much more up than down.

1. Sit in a chair with your feet square on the ground and your spine straight. This body posture helps the flow of your positive energy.

2. Close your eyes and take three big breaths slowly, in and out.

3. Now, on your inner mind-screen, imagine what a loving heart looks like.

4. Next, imagine that loving heart safely growing bigger and softer... as much you want... until it feels absolutely the right loving heart size for you.

5. Now, trusting your own Inner Wisdom, imagine yourself gently nestling in your big, soft and loving heart.

6. Give yourself time to feel whatever you feel nestling in it. These feelings are part of your mending process.

7. When you feel ready, let your loving heart with the image of you safely nestling in it merge into where your physical heart is. Notice how that feels.

8. Finally, when you feel ready, slowly turn your attention outward again. Notice the pressure of the chair against your body. Stretch your arms and move your legs. Become aware of the room and any noises around you. Then, very slowly open your eyes and come back into your room.

9. If you feel light-headed, roughly and quickly rub up and down your limbs, around your chest and belly. Finally, pat your face vigorously with both hands as if trying to wake yourself up. Repeat as necessary until you feel normal again.

This exercise helps many people to connect with the love and compassion they either have never felt or had stopped feeling in their depressed-ness.

You might have cried or even sobbed. You might also have felt relief that, at last, you felt some love and compassion, especially for yourself. Remember – you are enough.

If, by any chance, you got negative stuff then scrub it all out. You might well have stopped doing the exercise because of such feelings. This would be the anti-life gremlins playing tricks on you. Shame on them! Wait until you're feeling much better before using this exercise again.

If you have any questions about this exercise, please do email me sharon@bouncebackuk.com and I'll get back to you as soon as I can.

In conclusion

Action = achievement = lift your mood

Remember – do something. Do anything.

As well as lifting your mood, taking action – however little – will help rebuild your self-esteem, self-belief, confidence and resilience. These are excellent foundation stones from which to bounce back from depression.

GO DO IT!

11

NOW WHAT?

11

NOW WHAT?

Is depression likely to recur?

The simple answer is 'yes'. It seems, statistically, that when you've had one bout of depression you are likely to experience a further episode or episodes. But, hey, you might be the one to beat the statistics.

If not, the good news is you can learn to recognise the first signs of depression. When you do, you can do things to prevent depression deepening, find your personal development message and bring about bounce back.

Early signs for me are feelings of 'too much to do', a smidgeon of 'can't be bothered', and starting to not eat healthily. What are yours?

Some of what you can do to bounce back is in this book. With practice, those things will help you to not fall into the pit of despond when you feel yourself going down. The more you do to neutralise your anti-life energy gremlins, the quicker you recover.

Remember, you *can* bounce back from depression much sooner than the medical world suggests. Depression is part of the human condition and when we accept it as such, rather than being a 'victim' of an illness, movement and growth can happen.

Will I have depression forever?

I recently discovered someone I was working with had the idea that depression was always present and ready to go off like a firework show at the slightest thing. Not so!

Think of depression as being a part of your personality: just as other different parts of your personality have different roles in your life, whether you express them or not. So, just as you have stern parent, happy-go-lucky child, organised, disorganised, creative and practical parts, for example, you will also have a depressed part.

Is your parent or child part waiting to grab a piece of the action willy-nilly? Probably not. What's most likely is they only appear in your behaviour within certain contexts or environments.

It's exactly the same with depression. Prolonged stress provides a fertile context. Major life changes, losses, lack of meaning and purpose, and ongoing low self esteem, for example, also provide external/internal environments ripe for depression. Although that doesn't mean you will automatically experience depression, just that you might.

So, no. You don't 'have' depression forever. It's just a part of your personality which could be triggered in certain situations.

While starting to write this book...

I was under lots of pressure. My beloved brother-in-law died unexpectedly and suddenly in the January. So, I went over to America twice within a few months to support my sister in her bereavement.

At the same time, my business was disappearing due to organisational cutbacks in the recession. And my visits to the USA took a whole chunk of time out of my schedule which meant I couldn't stimulate more work. Consequently, I was getting into debt. 'Bag Lady' anti-life gremlins had a field day with me!

I returned from my second USA trip psychologically, emotionally and mentally depleted. Did I get depressed? You bet I got depressed.

So, when I say I'm a recovering depressive, I mean it. Just like an addict I need to be conscious of how I am one day at a time.

And so do you.

I was too busy to recognise the first signs of that last depression. Once I came out of the whirlwind and saw the signs, I took action to embrace my depression, begin my own personal bounce back and discover my personal development lesson.

In conclusion

Use this book as your guide to keep yourself healthy and to lift you up should you fall. While depression has gifts to offer you, you can learn how to reap them early and without descending into the darkness.

So, make sure you get enough sleep, eat healthy foods, mix with positive people... and don't stress yourself out of your box.

12

DEPRESSION'S GIFTS

12

DEPRESSION'S GIFTS

Once you have a solid recovery going, you can start exploring the learning opportunities your depression brought with it. Depression is always, but always, an opportunity for personal growth.

If you're feeling down, the anti-life energy gremlins will delight in giving you negative stuff. So only begin these exercises when your mood is generally more up than down.

What came before I got depressed?

This could be internal things, like worrying about something or feeling all alone, heartbreak, lack of confidence, feeling a fraud or not good enough. And/or, this could be external things, like severe work or relationship pressures, financial problems, a death, being in the wrong job, redundancy or any major life change..

What can I do to change those factors?

You will have no control over some of these, like a death or redundancy.

Most of the rest, though, depend on you. For example, with an unhappy relationship, one person will decide to seek help to make it better. Another will decide to end it. Another will decide to suffer in silence. Another will decide to accept things as they are.

Indeed, sometimes, acceptance of what is is the way to go. Remember the Serenity Prayer?

My preference these days is to do something where it's within my power to do it. Remember, action = achievement = lift your mood. However difficult it might be, if you can change the things which led to your depression, internal or external, please do.

What's my Soul trying to teach me?

Once you get an idea of what those depression triggers are, close your eyes, focus down into your belly, take three deep breaths and ask yourself, 'What's my Soul trying to teach me?' You might want to use others words there, like God, the Divine, my Inner Wisdom, Jesus, Buddha or Mohammed, blessed be he. Use whatever works for you.

Then, take whatever answers you get, even if they don't make sense or seem bizarre. You might get words, pictures, sounds, symbols, a memory or sensations.

Record whatever you get. If you don't yet understand what the teaching message is, trust your Inner Wisdom. In the following days or weeks you will realise what your answers mean.

As soon as you recognise you're experiencing depression, you can ask your Soul what it's trying to teach you. Sometimes people get the answer right away and take action, short-cutting the recovery process. If you don't, take heart. That doesn't happen all the time but it's always worth a go.

I wish I had a fairy wand

I could then tell you exactly what your depression's teaching message and learning gifts are. But I don't have that fairy wand. And your personal development through embracing depression is unique to you as it's the next step in your evolution as a human being.

All I can do is give you some examples from my life in the next section. See whether they stimulate any insights in you.

What are you going to do with your learning?

In my 30s and early 40s I had cycles of depressive episodes. When I finally got it, I realised there was a reason the Universe kept knocking on my door – and breaking it down.

Depression was telling me that being a respectable, middle class, suburban wife and mother was killing me. My learning was that I was not being/doing what I was being called to do in my life and work, including my marriage.

When I finally heard that gift, I was joyful, shaken and afraid. I was being asked to change much of my life in order to be truer to myself and, if you like, my job on earth. The only choice I could make was to take action in line with that message, however hard it was. And I did.

If I hadn't, nothing would have changed and I believe my depression would have continued to occur again and again. Only when you embrace depression and listen to its message can you recover and be free.

The learning of my most recent depression (after my USA trips) was that I was hooked on achieving glitzy ra-ra-ra success. What I was doing was full of ego and grandiosity. How I was behaving was at odds with who I really am. I was going in absolutely the wrong direction for me.

As hard as that was, too, I had no other choice but to listen to the voice of my Inner Wisdom and do an about turn. I now recognise the personality parts of me that can get hooked on grandiosity and keep them in check. I also listen more intently to my Inner Wisdom and its guidance.

The result of that depression was I launched Bounce-BackUK, am writing this book and loads more at peace with myself. Both feet are on the ground and I love the far softer and loving me which developed through the fire of my depression.

As sure as eggs are eggs, that will change. Life is an upward spiralling cycle of beginnings and endings. All are designed to help you and I evolve personally and spiritually.

We could, of course, hypothetically close our eyes and ears to it all. However, my experience is that once we start growing, there's no way back, I'm very glad to say.

You don't have to make such wide-ranging changes in response to your learning messages as I did. Or to make them all at the same time as I've done. I'm a very all or nothing woman!

You are likely to be different to me. So, let your own Inner Wisdom guide you as to what you do to make changes, how you make them and when you make them.

13

RESILIENCE

13

RESILIENCE

What is resilience?

Resilience is the ability to cope with adversity. It's an awesome by-product gift of depression which I've saved to last.

Having resilience means you're able to use your skills and strengths to cope better with life's curveballs. These include things like job loss, financial problems, physical illness, minor psychological dis-ease, natural or man-made disasters, medical emergencies, loss of a loved one, divorce and so on.

Resilience helps you to face problems head on, even if you feel like crap. It helps you move through your hard times creatively and make the best of how things turn out.

People without resilience can easily get overwhelmed. It seems they take longer to recover from a setback and experience more psychological distress. Depression, here I come.

Some people seem to have resilience as part of their personality. But maybe they had good early role models from whom they learned how to be resilient. Some other people, including me, learn resilience as an adult.

The #1 way I learned to be resilient was through:

- Learning how to recover from depression,

- Taking its gifts to learn what I needed to learn

- Making positive changes in myself and my life as a result.

Every time you do that, you build your resilience. This helps you to cope better with life's challenges *and* recover from depression more quickly than before.

Through using this book and moving yourself into recovery, you are learning to develop your resilience: the ability to cope with adversity.

That's an asset. It will make you more able to cope with the tough times if and when they come and enjoy life more.

Being in the 'now'

It's so easy to pull yourself down with obsessive negative thinking and feelings, usually about the past or future. I've mentioned before that enjoying the here and now, 'what is', is what matters in recovering from depression and general wellbeing.

It's also a part of resilience. Here's a simple technique to bring you back from negative thinking.

Clap your hands very loudly and quickly in front of your nose to bring you back into reality. Then think of three things for which you are grateful and enjoy. Take the first three things that come to mind. Here's my first three right now:

- Rock songs

- Clean laundry

- Mustard pickles

You can see they can be absolutely anything.

When you've had a go at this technique, where's your negative thinking gone?

Pro-life energy

As you develop resilience, you can deal with not-good things when they occur. There's also always lots of positive pro-life stuff around to support you. All you have to do is notice.

- A beautiful sunset

- The kind words of a stranger

- A favourite song or CD

- The smile of someone you love

- Getting earthy when gardening

- The support of a good friend

What's one positive pro-life thing in your life right now?

What you focus on grows

Whatever you focus on grows. So focus on the positive stuff rather than the negative pull-you-down stuff. And see how it grows day by day.

I recognised decades ago that I was a terrible moaner. Moan, moan and moan, day and night. I also woke up to the fact that I was creating misery for myself and others with all that moaning.

I would be lying if I said it all changed overnight. It didn't. But I eventually got to the point where, when I felt a moan coming on, I could choose not to. In the end, being moan-free became my new habit. That meant I could enjoy life more.

And sometimes I just choose to have a good moan anyway, usually five minutes' worth with a best friend. Containing it like that helps me let off steam in a safe and harmless way – and be done with it!

An attitude of gratitude

An attitude of gratitude helps too. This is not a Pollyanna, happy-clappy, everything's-perfect-when-it-isn't attitude. An attitude of gratitude enables you to be thankful for the good things in your life even when the going is tough.

And, not surprisingly, those good things multiply the more you are grateful for them. Remember? What you focus on always, but always, increases.

The learning

A REMINDER THAT, EVEN THOUGH IT SEEMS IMPOSSIBLE RIGHT NOW, DEPRESSION ALWAYS COMES WITH A GIFT, LEARNING FOR YOUR PERSONAL DEVELOPMENT, HIDDEN IN ITS SHADOWS.

And the more you embrace your depression, the more likely you are to find it.

Don't beat yourself up if you don't find that learning right away. You'll realise your gift at some point. That often happens when you're not looking for it. Keep a small notebook and pen available at all times so you can record your gift before it slips away, as insights often do.

One day you'll say something like, 'If it wasn't for depression, I wouldn't be running my own business', or 'I wouldn't be in a loving relationship' or 'I wouldn't be living here.' That might seem ludicrous right now. But please send me an email when it's your turn to say something similar.

And, for now, all you have to do is take one baby step at a time, using every tip in this book you can. I do it. My clients do it. And so can you.

YOU *CAN* BOUNCE BACK FROM DEPRESSION –
AND MUCH SOONER THAN YOU THINK

Go well and gently.

INSPIRATIONAL QUOTATIONS

'Too much of a good thing can be wonderful.'
Mae West

'No matter how dark things seem to be... raise your sights and see possibilities... they're always there.'
Norman Vincent Peale

'A positive attitude may not serve all your problems, but it will annoy enough people to make it worth the effort.'
Herm Albright

'The best way out is always through.'
Robert Frost

'Whatever you can do, or dream you can, begin it. Boldness has genius, power and magic in it!'
Johann Wolfgang von Goethe

'We need to set our course by the stars, not by the lights of every passing ship.'
Olmar N Bradley

'The difference between winning and
losing is most often… not quitting.'

Walt Disney

'If you obey all the rules, you miss all the fun.'

Katharine Hepburn

'Take advantage of opportunity even
when it looks like adversity.'

Jeffrey Gitomer

'Listen: We are here on earth to fart around.
Don't let anybody tell you any different!'

Kurt Vonnegut Jr

'I am here to live out loud.'

Emile Zola

'Very often a change of self is needed
more than a change of scene.'

Arthur Christopher Benson

'When you change, the world around you changes.'

Niurka

'Only those who dare to fall greatly
can ever achieve greatly.'

John Kennedy

'A champion is one who gets up even when he can't.'

Jack Dempsey

'Nurture your mind with great thoughts,
for you will never go any higher than you think.'

Benjamin Disraeli

'It is of immense importance to
learn to laugh at ourselves.'

Katherine Mansfield

'So what do we do? Anything – something.
So long as we don't just sit there.'

Lee Iacocca

'When the going gets tough, the tough get going.'

Joseph P Kennedy

'Be the change you want to see in the world.'

Mahatma Ghandi

'Our greatest glory is not in never falling,
but in rising every time we fall.'

Confucius

'Whether you think you can
or think you can't, you're right.'

Henry Ford

'We are not human beings having a spiritual
experience; we are spiritual beings having
a human experience.'

Pierre de Teilhard de Chardin

'You don't have to see the whole staircase,
just take the first step.'

Martin Luther King Jr

'When God closes a door, he opens a window.'

Origin unknown

ACKNOWLEDGEMENTS

To all my teachers throughout life, I give my thanks. Special thanks to those at the Psychosynthesis and Education Trust who offered me a bedrock for myself and my profession.

Thanks especially to my courageous and inspiring clients for the privilege of working with them. You are my very special teachers.

My thanks to anyone who's ever helped me believe in myself and my purpose. From Mrs Levy, my junior school teacher, to Andrew; my wonderful Wizard women buddies, and long-time friends, Irene, Lise, Phyllis, Sharon and Frances.

Adam and Cassie, my children, thank you for your unswerving backing and belief in me, your encouragement and great humour... even when you thought me off the wall.

Lastly, thanks to Lucy McCarraher and all at Rethink Press for their guidance and expertise. Without you *Bounce Back from Depression* would not have been born so alive and kicking.

THE AUTHOR

Sharon Eden is the Depression Coach and helps people recover from depression within six sessions or less. She calls herself a 'recovering depressive,' having spent earlier decades battling depression and suicidal episodes. And she is passionate about helping people to recover *and* sustain their recovery.

In another life, Sharon worked in corporate sales and marketing and education. During a psychology degree and training as a psychotherapist in the 1980s, she determined to research and develop techniques which would *really* help her and others to recover. Her ongoing work has culminated in a groundbreaking and holistic paradigm for depression and its treatment.

Sharon is delighted that her credentials include an MA (Psychotherapy) awarded when she was 51. They also include being a Registered Member, Association for Counselling and Psychotherapy (Accredited); Member, Association of Integrative Coach-Therapist Professionals; Member, Applied Psychology Association; and Member, International Positive Psychology Association.

Her earlier book, *Whack Around The Head – Purpose, Passion and Power at Work Right Now!* is full of insights and exercises to help people become happier at work. Her vision for *Bounce Back* includes training courses in her innovative model of depression and treatment. These will be both for professionals and people who want to become 'recovering depressives' just like her.

You can learn more about Sharon at
www.bouncebackuk.com and...

Twitter	@sharoneden
Facebook	www.facebook.com/sharoneden.biz
LinkedIn	Sharon Eden
Google Plus	Sharon Eden
Pinterest	www.pinterest.com/BounceBackUK/

14038990R00094

Printed in Great Britain
by Amazon.co.uk, Ltd.,
Marston Gate.